The work of FXFOWLE is characterized by an approach to architecture that views buildings as part of the larger scale of nature. From the scale of the building to the scale of infrastructure to the scale of the city, we integrate architecture, building systems, and natural systems. Connections to nature, whether cultural or experiential, are critically important to our thought process. The architectural expression resonates with nature and brings the experience of landscape to constructed space and the experience of constructed space to landscape.

Our architecture is based on two coincidental beliefs: that culture emerges from nature and that nature is defined by culture. The two cannot be separated. Our practice exemplifies these convictions, and the content of our design work speaks directly to the role of the environment. We attempt to work in concert with nature; to engage science, measurement, and advanced technology to protect resources; and to bring the ideas and methodologies of landscape into our practice.

The projects in this volume reveal the territory between architecture and landscape. Design strategies juxtapose, extend, and blur this threshold space, and techniques of expression and form commingle with approaches to sustainability and natural systems. The landscape and ecological tendencies that provide the context for our work are integrated within our work. The architecture is porous, blurring boundaries, extending margins, erasing divisions, fostering coherence and balance.

At the **Center for Global Conservation** at the Bronx Zoo, the landscape rises to the building, and the interior extends to the landscape. Shaped as much by its natural

context as by its program, the structure expresses the dynamic forces of landscape, realizing a unity of building and site, an inextricable whole.

The **Qala Alti Hotel Spa** in Azerbaijan is a conversation between built form and mountain terrain. Building typologies and material palettes are drawn from the landscape, unveiling the connections between architecture and nature. The design revels in ambiguities and simultaneously offers moments of clarity.

Interdependent building systems work seamlessly with natural systems at the **SAP Americas Headquarters Expansion** in Pennsylvania. The means of operating the building—interactive heating, cooling, and ventilation—create a flexible interior environment. A strong, sweeping form that fits instinctively into its setting, the building elicits an experience of sustainability, an active engagement that changes the way that the architecture is perceived.

The **Sheikh Rashid bin Saeed Crossing** in Dubai both connects and transforms the urban context. The massive bridge, a bifurcated arch that touches down in the middle of Dubai Creek, joins the city to the fabric of the landscape. On the banks of the waterway and on Bridge Creek Island, we have constructed an ecology that interacts with the tidal waterway.

A competition entry for a sustainable city for the twenty-first century, **City Regenerative: Nordhavnen** conceives of landscape and architecture as two halves of a whole. The urban organism—an ecology of infrastructure, buildings, and open space—optimizes natural resources

in a far-reaching display of sustainable thinking. A green infrastructure is legible and celebrated; a green urbanism integrates building and natural systems.

The inherent humanism that underlies our work reflects a desire for an architecture that balances the experience of its users with the responsibilities of intervening in a greater context. Exploring the liminal space between architecture and landscape energizes design not through a static image or composition but through a fluid experience. We take notice of the building in use, emphasizing circulation and layout, reconfiguring program relationships, implementing building systems that allow for individual control, and using materials that evoke a connection with the larger world. These design strategies put on equal footing the experience of the interior and the expression of the exterior, revealing the interrelation between humankind and nature and advancing a greater stewardship of the environment.

Nature as Site
Kent Kleinman

Kent Kleinman is the Gale
and Ira Drukier Dean of
Cornell University's College of
Architecture, Art, and Planning.

In the Western artistic canon, it has long been commonplace
that serious contemplation of the human condition is separate
from, and superior to, considerations of nature. The most noble
of artistic pursuits was the depiction of narrative subjects from
mythology or the Bible. In contrast, the lowest echelon of artistic
subject matter was the depiction of nature. Alberti had grave
doubts about expending creative effort on representing nature,
writing that landscape views, though they provided a kind
of innocent delight, lacked the didactic and moral content
of the highest form of art, the representation of *historia*. Art historian
Peter Sutton neatly summarized the hierarchy of subject matter
during the Renaissance: "Landscapes appealed to the eye
but not the intellect."[1] Indeed, the genre of landscape painting
was fairly well dismissed as a minor art form, at best a pleasant
divertimento, at worst an abuse of the intellect. Humanist scholar
and artist Dominicus Lampsonius claimed that the artist
preoccupied with depicting nature had his "brains in his hands."[2]

1   Peter Sutton, *Masters of
Seventeenth-Century Dutch
Landscape Painting* (Boston:
Museum of Fine Arts, 1987), 8.

2   Cited in Ernst Gombrich,
*Norm and Form: Studies in the
Art of the Renaissance* (London:
Phaidon, 1966), 115.

Pieter van Santvoort,
*Landscape with
Farmhouse and
Country Road,* 1625

Who were these artists that earned such disdain, these artists with empty heads and soiled hands? They were, for the most part, the Dutch. If the genre of landscape depiction has a single home, it is the Netherlands, especially the Netherlands of the Golden Age. During this time, images of the land proliferated to a degree unprecedented in Western art. The very term "landscape" is derived from the Dutch *landtschap*. Never before had the land been so privileged as the subject of artistic scrutiny; never before had it been depicted with such apparent dedication to veracity and devotion to detail; and never before had images of the land found such a voracious market. The reason for this perverse preoccupation is clear: never before had nature been so thoroughly conceptualized as the raw material of nation building. For during the late sixteenth and early seventeenth centuries, the Dutch provinces were literally constructing their nationhood.

The extensive reclamation projects of the Golden Age are now legend. During this period the northern provinces more than doubled their terrain by erecting dikes around inland lakes and ejecting the water with wind-powered pumps, winning vast tracts of productive land. The scale of the reclamation works was unprecedented in human history and produced a new kind of commoditized and instrumental geography. Bleaching fields, peat bogs, agricultural plots, and building sites: all were raised up into the service of a nation that needed to establish a stable physical presence on earth. These territories were laced together by a network of linear canals and serviced by ferries that bridged the centers of commerce and culture, making the construction of the terrain synonymous with the construction of a national identity. The Dutch knowledge of shaping land was so advanced that it even served as a military weapon. When the Spanish laid siege to Leiden in the 1570s, for instance, the Dutch breached the surrounding dikes, flooded the polder, and launched flat-bottomed boats to rescue the city. Later in the conflict, the Dutch dealt a decisive blow to the Spanish by stopping up the mouth of the Scheldt River, diverting trade from Catholic Antwerp to Protestant Amsterdam. The Dutch concept of the "ground" possessed a degree of plasticity, malleability, instrumentality, and formal potential that is not typically associated with the term "nature." The Dutch were not "grounded" in a given, natural environment; instead, they inhabited an earthscape largely of their own devising and dwelt in a nature of their own design.

We are increasingly required to accept such a concept of nature and embrace such a vast scope of operation for our acts of design. I write this with trepidation and delight, for it means that we have no choice but to be responsible for shaping our own nature. If it were once thought that architects site their buildings, we now know that we always also build the site, recalibrating visible and invisible ecological systems. This condition has been eloquently described by the contemporary French philosopher Bruno Latour, who noted that what we once categorized as constants—matters of fact we can observe, measure, and analyze but not influence

3   Bruno Latour, "A Cautious Prometheus? A Few Steps Toward a Philosophy of Design (with Special Attention to Peter Sloterdijk)," in *Proceedings of the 2008*

Annual International Conference of the Design History Society, ed. Fiona Hackne, Jonathn Glynne, and Viv Minto (Falmouth: Universal Publishers, 2009), 2–10.

to any significant degree—have now become variables in the calculus of human activity.[3] Latour refers specifically to climate change: with few exceptions, the scientific community is in agreement that climate is a matter of fact no more but a matter of debate, policy formation, and deliberate action, in short, a matter of design.

The representation of nature in the projects of FXFOWLE is noteworthy. The images are not immune from the representational conventions that nestle the crisp edges of architectural artifice among the soft verdant foliage of vegetation, as if these were two ontologically distinct worlds. This is a long and distinguished visual trope: even the seventeenth-century Dutch had a hard time foregrounding the actuality of their constructed environments, favoring images of wild rivers when in truth their waters ran straight, and of aged forests when in truth there were few trees that they had not planted. The desire to represent nature as given runs deep. But the projects in this volume show that change is in the air. FXFOWLE is at the forefront of a movement that is systematically dissolving the boundary between the built and the natural, deliberately embracing a new scope for the designer and inventing formal strategies that produce environments as much as they shape individual buildings. While this ambition runs through a great number of the projects featured here, nowhere is it more clearly demonstrated than in the competition scheme for Nordhavnen, which refuses any sentimental dialogue between sea and land, yoking the habitation of the recycled site to the performative capacities of the surrounding elements.

The principals of FXFOWLE often use this project to demonstrate their commitment to, and remarkable facility with, sustainable urbanism, correctly noting that urban form is a critical dimension of sustainable design. But the evocation of the term "urban" tends to evoke its binary counterpart, the rural/natural. Perhaps the Nordhavnen project is more profound, more total. For if climate is a matter of design, a *site*, what of nature is not?

CENTER FOR GLOBAL CONSERVATION
BRONX, NEW YORK, 2009, WILDLIFE CONSERVATION SOCIETY
43,500 SQUARE FEET, LEED GOLD

When you think about blurring the edges of a building into the landscape, you are more sensitive to how a building is inhabited and experienced, as well as to how it performs. The building and its landscape become one. Sylvia Smith

The Wildlife Conservation Society, parent organization of five zoos in New York City, works to save wildlife and wild lands and manages outreach programs and missions around the world. The Center for Global Conservation, headquarters for the WCS, is sited on the northern edge of the Bronx Zoo. The environmentally-responsible building, which embodies the organization's mission and provides a supportive and enriching work environment, houses the departments for international programs, exhibition and graphic design, and information technology, once scattered around the 256-acre zoo campus. The synergy between the activist mission of the WCS and our dedication to principles of responsible and responsive design energized the design process and informed a rich dialogue between client and architect and between building and landscape.

   The long, low building embraces and frames its natural setting. The strong, unadorned form merges with the site; exterior spaces expand the interior. The play of light, careful balance of scale and proportion, framing of views, and use of natural materials establish a poetic resonance between building and landscape. The immediacy of the overall composition and the awareness of nature and its rhythms enhance occupant well-being and define a unique sense of place.

   The contours of the site—two rock outcroppings running from north to south with a hollow in between, a meadow to the south, and a constructed lake to the north—suggest the warp and weft of woven fabric. We modeled the landscape in tandem with the building, using the architecture to cradle and define an intimate space. The entry sequence begins at the south edge of the site, where we "lifted" the landscape and inserted a gate of concrete panels. The promenade leads through the meadow, paralleling the rock outcroppings. Pushed down in the center, the meadow has been transformed into a wetland that accumulates and filters water that runs through the site. At the north, the meadow forecourt rises to meet and merge with the CGC.

The building was shaped around an existing stand of trees. A narrow form stretching from east to west, maximizing daylight and views. The connection between landscape and architecture is expressed in its orientation, scale, circulation, materials, and details. The spatial sequence within the center and the weaving of landscape and structure allow staff and visitors to pass effortlessly between interior and exterior. An emphasis on sightlines and pathways makes the building feel larger than its footprint might indicate. The flow of the spaces and the views from inside to outside extend the building into the landscape.

The promenade across the site continues within the building as a series of spaces punctuated by light. Outdoor landscapes at different levels are paired with interior areas. A green roof planted with native perennials climbs the face of the building, creating a zone that is both architecture and constructed landscape. On the interior, the elevated ground plane is mirrored by a sloping ceiling that defines the exhibition design studio. Exposed structural elements—concrete columns and beams—reinforce the building's essential and unadorned character.

A compact lobby leads to a second-floor gathering space. A few steps away is a large glass-enclosed meeting room that sits among the trees atop the east outcrop. Meeting room and gathering space share an exterior deck. As part of an ongoing effort to reduce bird strikes, the meeting room is sheathed in a recently developed, UV-treated glass that is more visible to birds. The path through the building continues to a conference room on the third floor. An adjoining terrace, which connects with the ramped green roof, transports occupants into the site both physically and perceptually.

The allocation of spaces for work, assembly, and circulation fosters interaction between staff, among visitors, and with the landscape. Flexible open areas provide work space for employees, as well as for a steady flow of visiting researchers and dignitaries. These workstations are located on the south side of the building, maximizing natural lighting. Private offices, limited in number, are situated on the north side.

A refined approach to materials and proportion, one that emphasizes natural elements and human dimensions, guided the design. Red sandstone salvaged from the Lion House in the zoo's historic Astor Court is used for panels on both exterior and interior, a subtle link between the past and present of the WCS. Continuous floor and ceiling planes, the intimate glass entry, and authentic materials reinforce the continuity between interior and exterior. A sunshade on the south side of the building, made of sustainably harvested black locust, is a rustic counterpoint to the sleek glass and concrete. Trees that were cleared from the site were milled into wood trim that was installed throughout the building.

We designed the building to maximize passive strategies for natural ventilation and reduced energy and water use. The shape, organization, fenestration, systems, and controls lessen demand for resources and also enhance life within. Heating and cooling is distributed through an underfloor system. Individual controls and operable windows allow staff members to manage their personal comfort. A microturbine cogeneration miniplant produces the building's electricity.

The building and the landscape are bound together, as are the building and its high purpose: one cannot exist without the other. Attention to the specifics of the environment fostered an abundance of natural light and views; an open layout and inside/outside meeting spaces support collaborative work; and materials and sustainable strategies connect building occupants to their mission. This cohesion of architecture and nature goes beyond building logic. It infuses the building with a poetic dimension and a unique sense of place. Each element plays a part; removal of a single part compromises the whole. The unified composition of building and landscape captures an equally unified fusion of unique location and noble aspiration.

Existing Site

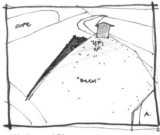

Lift Ground Plan

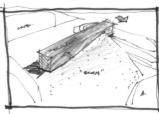

Insert Program

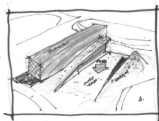

Cut Landscape

Site

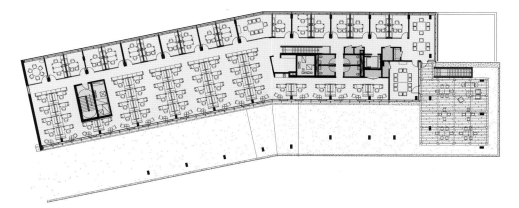

Third Floor Plan

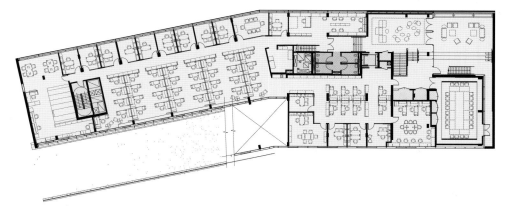

Second Floor Plan

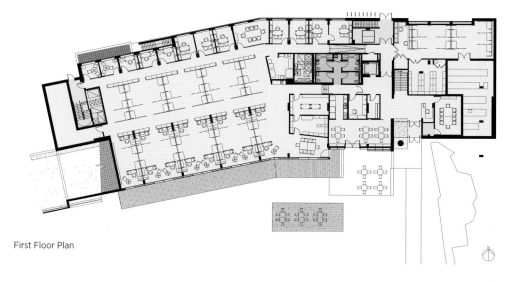

First Floor Plan

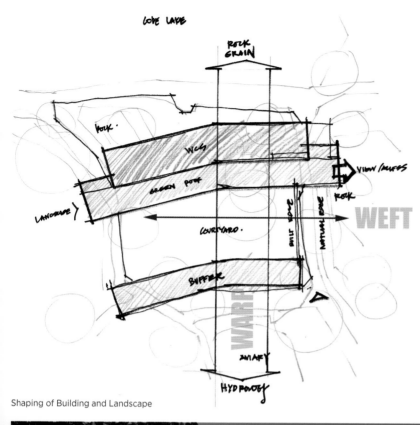

Shaping of Building and Landscape

1   Gathering Space

2   Main Entry

3   Conference Room

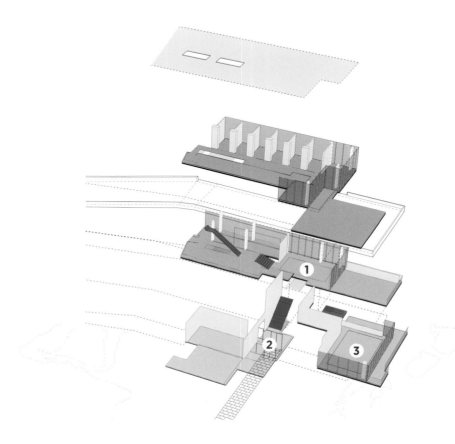

Although it is vital to embrace sustainable practices in the design of individual buildings, it is the density of cities and their deep-seated relationship to built and natural systems that creates the most sustainable condition. The way we dwell, the way we travel, and the way we share resources make it impossible to consider the micro scale without the macro scale. Dan Kaplan and Mark Strauss

A competition for the Nordhavnen district of Copenhagen offered the opportunity to envision a truly sustainable city—a city where urbanism, architecture, and all residential, professional, and recreational pursuits would come together in a fusion of natural systems, urban infrastructure, and responsible building. The new district is expected to house 40,000 residents, create 40,000 jobs, and provide access for 40,000 bicycles. Our proposal, City Regenerative, connects urban infrastructure, extends the existing waterway, and weaves open space through a series of neighborhoods and commercial nodes. Nordhavnen is close to the historic center of Copenhagen, but only a fragment of the site currently exists. The land itself will be constructed over time from the tailings of a railroad tunnel currently under construction.

Our approach to urban planning abides by Eliel Saarinen's directive to "always design a thing by considering it in its next larger context—a chair in a room, a room in a house, a house in an environment, an environment in a city plan." Here the larger context is the Danish coast, particularly Copenhagen's canal system. We created a central canal that extends Copenhagen's central Sydhavnen Canal as the organizing spine for the new district. The neighborhoods of City Regenerative span the canal and are composed around a secondary network of waterways and open spaces. The intersections between each neighborhood and the central canal are marked by bridges and canal towers. A matrix of greenways mixed with transit and waterways offers convenient access to multiple modes of transportation, open space, parks, natural areas, neighborhood services, and the harbor.

To devote as much space as possible to open green areas, to create a walkable environment, and to promote the use of mass transit, we proposed a concentrated mix of uses. Each neighborhood comprises housing, institutions, commercial enterprises, and local parks. Low-rise canal houses line the waterfront; mid-rise courtyard houses disposed in relation to the canal houses delineate a zone of small parks; and high-rise towers stand within larger neighborhood parks. Nearly all units have views of canals or park areas, and all are integrated into the natural landscape and drainage system.

The main transit boulevard, interwoven with commercial nodes, transit hubs, and urban plazas, laces through the community, and a light-rail transit system parallels the central canal. Major transit plazas are situated at the intersections between neighborhoods, giving access to the water, bicycle storage, and nearby automated garages. These plazas facilitate transfers between foot, bike, tram, boat, and automobile.

The bridges across the canals provide important civic space but, more significant, accommodate "green towers" that provide all infrastructural services for Nordhavnen. These towers, the tallest features on the skyline, are organic in form and line the central canal. They provide structural support for the canal bridges and house gravity-fed water pumping stations, sea-water heat exchangers, district heating plants, and waste management hubs. Upper levels are devoted to vertical community farms. Lower levels furnish water treatment plants, collection points for waste and recycling, and heating and cooling plants. Farmer's markets are poised in between, at bridge level.

In the northeasternmost precinct of the newly constructed territory is a regionally scaled urban park, the culmination of the system of open space and the result of the overall strategy of density. The green space will develop into a wild and natural landscape that supports a wide range of species. Its jetties and coves will mirror the natural landscape of Denmark, with stretches of dunes, wooded groves, and grasslands extending into the sea.

Like the planning for the city, the tectonic system for Nordhavnen is developed with a view to inherent rather than applied sustainability. New buildings, whether residential, commercial, or institutional, utilize the Global Building Module technique of modular construction. The basic unit is prefabricated to match the size of an ISO shipping container. The modules lock together to form long structural spans. Fabrication plants for the modular system are located on site, providing employment for residents and earning Nordhavnen the moniker "the city that builds itself."

The three principles behind our design—housing density, connection to historic Copenhagen, modularity—produce a new form of sustainable urbanism that respects the patterns of postwar development in Denmark. But the concept goes further. Integrating urban footprint and natural systems, landscape and seascape, City Regenerative blurs built and existing, city and nature. The various systems will change and adapt as the new community is brought into being. City Regenerative is not a static dictum but a strategy and prescription for growth.

Land

Land: 1850

Land: 1900

Land: 1950

Land: 2000

Land: 2020

Land: 2035

Land: 2055

Evolution of Land/Water Edge

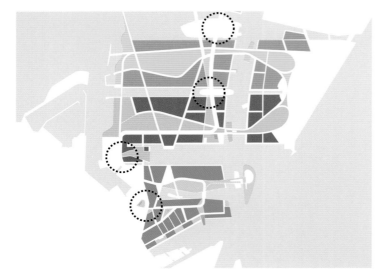

Districts

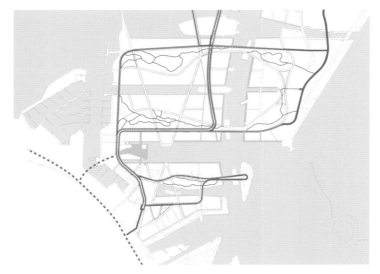

Bike

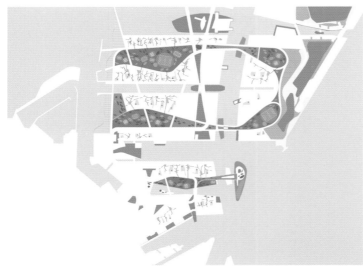

Green Space

Program

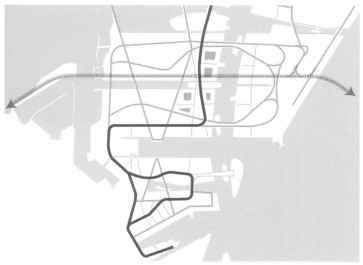

Vehicle

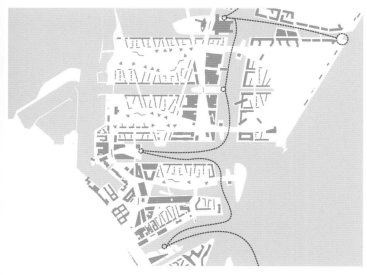

Water

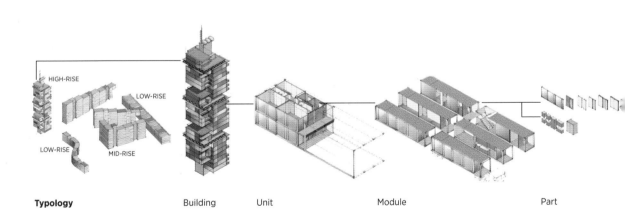

Typology   Building   Unit   Module   Part

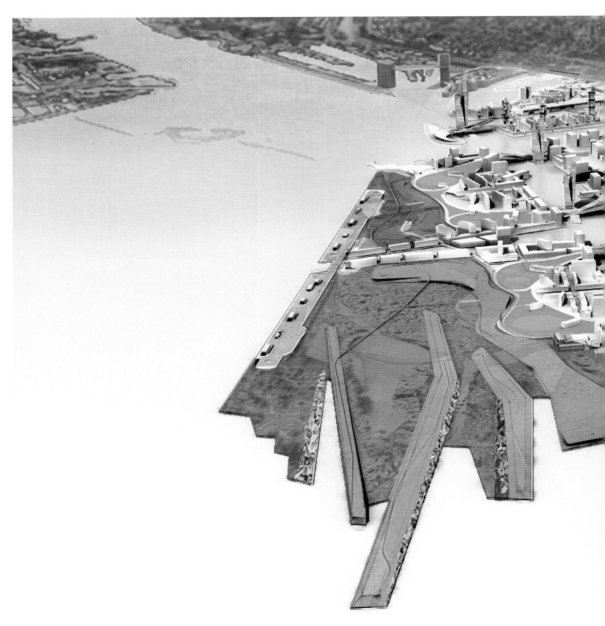

What is interesting about all the sustainable projects we have done is that they create a real connection between the building occupant and the environment. You are a participant with the building and with its regular activities. Guy Geier

The SAP Americas Headquarters Expansion is a tour-de-force of sustainable building systems. SAP, an environmentally-responsible German software company, organized a limited competition for an addition to its campus in the suburbs of Philadelphia. We proposed a high-performance building in which "good guts" influence form. Sustainability systems create interdependencies between site, energy and water use, materials and resources, indoor air quality, and well-being.

The building may be considered a living machine, one that improves the day-to-day existence of its inhabitants. And like a machine, the building can be "operated." This holistic approach to environmental architecture—in form, layout and circulation, design details, mechanical systems, and operations—tangibly embodies sustainability.

The existing headquarters, a gently curved structure of three stories, is surrounded by woodlands and the remnants of an arboretum. The expansion, two components that are connected by an atrium and form a reverse S, nestles into the land north of the original structure. A stand of specimen chestnut trees, the topography of the property, and the course of the sun all inflected the site plan. The land falls away from the existing building; the first floor of the addition is one level lower than the first floor of the old headquarters. Between the two are an outdoor garden and entry area. The integration of building and landscape corresponds with the linked building systems that make the most of the attributes of the local environment.

Lining the south facade of the new building is a generous atrium. This three-story circulation spine together with the new garden forms an inviting indoor-outdoor room that accommodates individual workers, casual meetings, and more formal events. The atrium admits natural light into the building but is deep enough to shield the work spaces on the north side from direct sun. Floor-to-ceiling laminated wood in the atrium—composed of FSC timber and sustainable glues—creates a sense of warmth and scale.

The expansion provides eight hundred workstations, conference rooms for the same number, and private offices. Closed offices and conference rooms are used to define "neighborhoods" of open-plan work areas; furniture and fittings from another SAP location were repurposed, minimizing material waste. The flexible arrangement allows SAP to modify the work space in response to changing business requirements. The office design emphasizes visual and physical connection to the landscape. Workstation neighborhoods have natural light and ventilation in both directions— through the atrium to the south and over pastoral woodland to the north. Accessible green roofs offer physical access to the landscape.

The building systems at SAP have carefully designed interdependencies that maximize efficiency. We worked with mechanical and structural engineers and landscape architects to bring together conventional and sustainable systems. Passive strategies for energy conservation include building orientation, shading, natural ventilation, triple glazing, and green roofs. The green roofs also collect stormwater, which is used to feed heating and cooling systems. Active mechanical systems—ice storage tanks, underfloor air, and radiant and geothermal heating— supplement the passive efforts.

We evaluated the sustainable systems for many criteria, including cost. While triple glazing was more expensive than double glazing, it allowed perimeter heating to be eliminated; thereby reducing up-front costs. We also looked for synergies between building systems. The open interior layout and an unorthodox use of smoke purge fans (a code requirement), along with operable windows, promote natural ventilation.

Design choices that improve air quality, employee well-being, and building function contribute to an experience of sustainability that is physically perceptible. Flexible and uninterrupted work areas with full-height glass windows, easy access to green roofs and the courtyard garden, and visual connection to the woodland outside generate an immersive setting for building users. But the expansion is responsive to the needs of occupants beyond physical access. Blinds automatically adjust to daylight, and the underfloor air system allows individuals to regulate the temperature in the immediate vicinity. The building expresses the ability of architecture to act, to perform through linked systems. Such performance has a positive impact not only on the natural environment but on the day-to-day lives of those who work within.

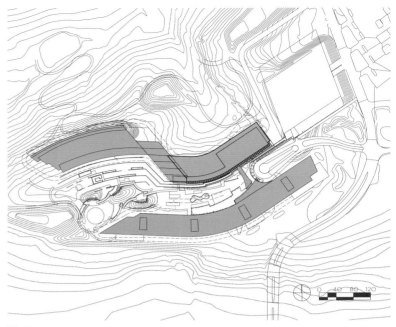

Site Plan

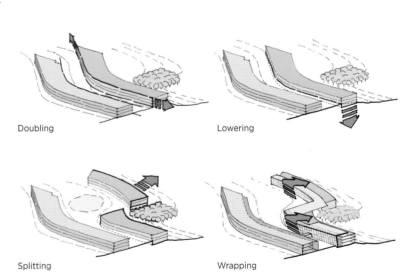

Doubling

Lowering

Splitting

Wrapping

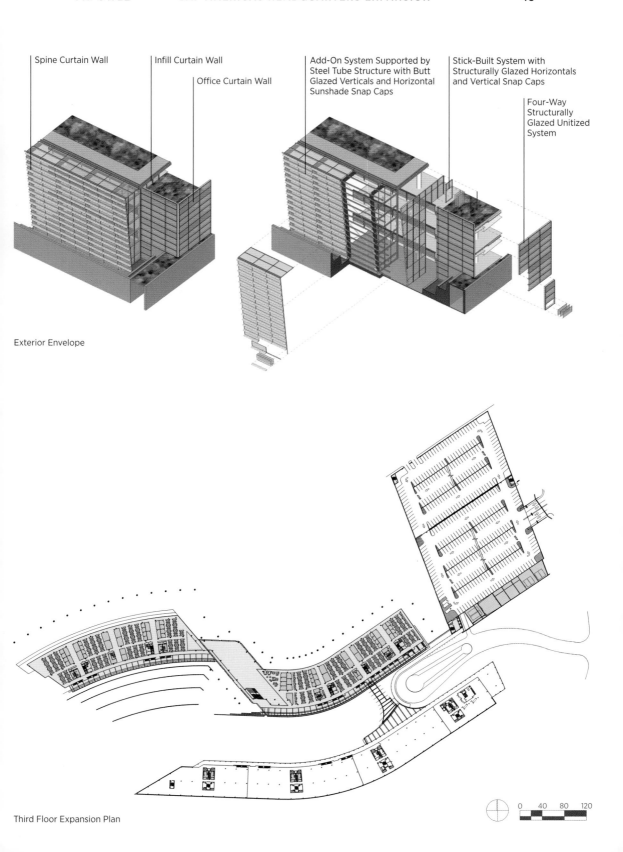

Spine Curtain Wall

Infill Curtain Wall

Office Curtain Wall

Add-On System Supported by Steel Tube Structure with Butt Glazed Verticals and Horizontal Sunshade Snap Caps

Stick-Built System with Structurally Glazed Horizontals and Vertical Snap Caps

Four-Way Structurally Glazed Unitized System

Exterior Envelope

Third Floor Expansion Plan

0   40   80   120

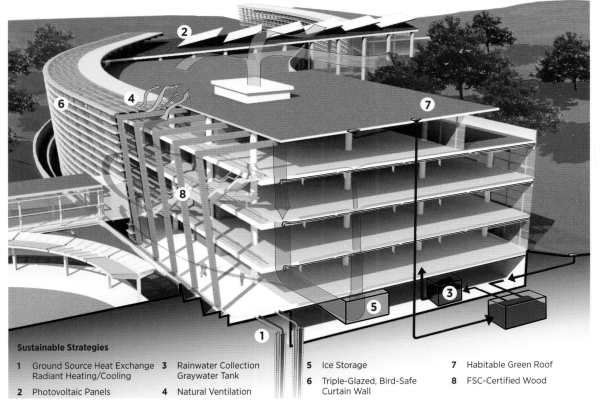

Sustainable Strategies

1	Ground Source Heat Exchange Radiant Heating/Cooling	**3**	Rainwater Collection Graywater Tank	**5**	Ice Storage	**7**	Habitable Green Roof
2	Photovoltaic Panels	**4**	Natural Ventilation	**6**	Triple-Glazed, Bird-Safe Curtain Wall	**8**	FSC-Certified Wood

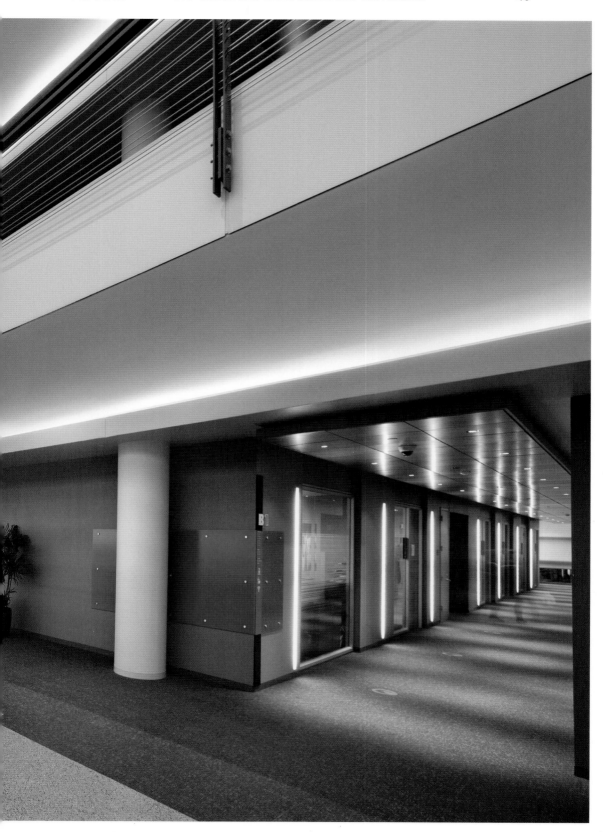

All projects we design connect to their surroundings. Whether the project is a bridge or a building or an urban master plan, we always establish connections. The idea of connection has two facets. The first is cultural: we connect whatever we design culturally. The second is physical: we connect through landscape or architecture. Sudhir Jambhekar

Sheikh Rashid bin Saeed Crossing (informally, Sixth Crossing) is an icon in a city of icons. The winner of an invited international design competition, the bridge is intended to alleviate traffic in the city of Dubai. 1.05 miles long and 282 feet wide, the bridge supports twelve lanes of automobile traffic as well as pedestrian and bicycle lanes and light rail, and it incorporates Bridge Creek Island, a newly constructed island with a covered amphitheater, public green spaces, exhibition center focusing on the local ecology, and ferry and light-rail stations.

The bridge spans Dubai Creek, which separates the ancient area of Jadaf in the Bur Dubai historic district from new developments to the east—the Lagoons and Festival City. The creek is an intertidal waterway that originates in the Arabian Gulf to the north of the city and flows south to swampy marshes. Dubai formed around the creek as an ancient trading city, and the creek is still used for merchant ships as well as tourist boats and a new ferry system. Sixth Crossing and Bridge Creek Island offer open spaces for recreation and will provide a gateway to wildlife areas to the south, including the Ras al Khor Wildlife Sanctuary.

We tested various basic bridge forms—suspension, cable-stay, box girder, and arch—always with an eye to fluidity and elegance. The virtues of the arch stood out. It looks to local culture—to the flowing gestures of Arabic calligraphy, the layered beauty of sand dunes, and the crescent moon—and is brilliant in its structural simplicity. We introduced a counternarrative of asymmetry to animate the figure and also to frame the proposed Zaha Hadid-designed Opera House on Opera Island. The two halves of the bridge are unequal in size, and the larger of the two components is itself asymmetrical. Sectional variations in the arched supports compensate for the unequal transfer of loads. Because of the scale of the bridge, concrete is used for the feet of the arches; the remainder of the supports is made of steel.

A great number of functions are incorporated into the bridge, creating a kind of sustainable infrastructure. It is a massive travelway for cars, with six lanes of traffic in each direction. A light rail line facilitates efficient transportation. The platform, in the center of the bridge, serves both directions, reducing the overall width of the station as well as the number of stairs, elevators, and escalators. Pedestrians and cyclists cross the bridge on a shaded walkway under the main deck. Mist machines give rise to a comfortable microclimate.

The ecological landscape of Sixth Crossing is envisaged as a threshold between the urban and the natural. Landscaped edges are inserted wherever land meets tidal waters—on the east and west banks and around the new island. Each area will give rise to a different tidal environment supporting unique plant and animal habitats. These native ecosystems will thrive with very little water. Hardscape materials are light in color to minimize the heat-island effect.

The west landing, which borders the navigation channel, has steeper slopes and more upland areas and nurtures upland and lowland groves. The east landing is more gently sloped. A shaded boardwalk traverses a lagoon landscape with reed beds and local *sabkhas* (salt flats). Bridge Creek Island supports a brackish, salt marsh environment. Pathways from the transportation hub travel through a misted forest to the tidal landscape. The various ecological systems will lure many species of birds to the area of Sixth Crossing.

The graceful and bold form of the bridge, part infrastructure and part landscape—or infrastructure at the scale of landscape—is infused with cultural and physical connections to Dubai. Even the night lighting, which increases as the moon waxes and dims as the moon wanes, refers to the Arabic lunar calendar. The constructed ecologies on the island advance the passage from steel structure to living systems. The crossing and the island also become part of the urban landscape, representing a transition between built form and the larger landscape context.

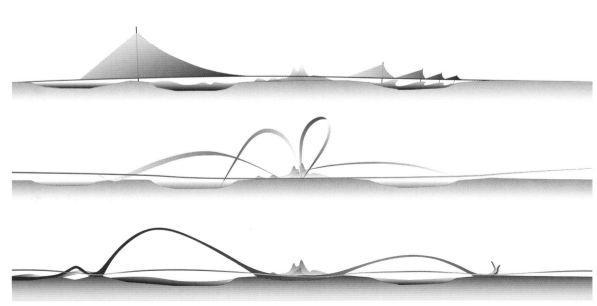

Concept Design Schemes

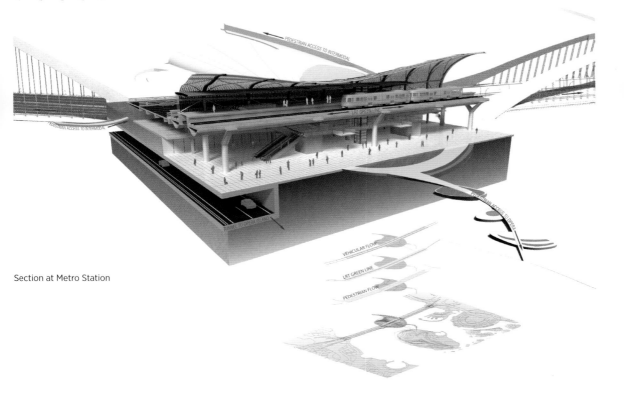

Section at Metro Station

Bridge Plan

Original Vertical Alignment

Proposed Vertical Alignment

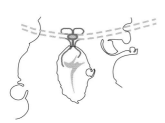

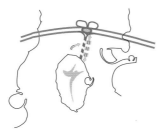

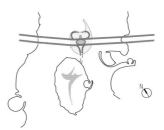

Original Plan

- Bridge gravitates toward Opera Island
- Road interchange is highly visible

First Option Plan

- More separation between bridge and Opera Island
- Road interchange remains highly visible but rotates in plan to open views to Opera House
- Lengthy tunnel required to reach Opera Island

Final Proposed Plan

- Straightened bridge alignment
- Road interchange partially buried to access Opera Island via tunnel
- Proposed island with direct pedestrian access to Opera House

Pedestrian Bridge

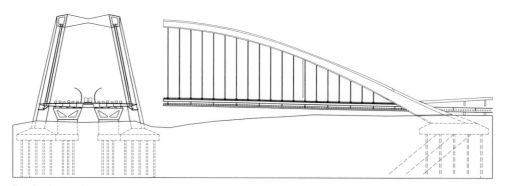

East Section and Elevation

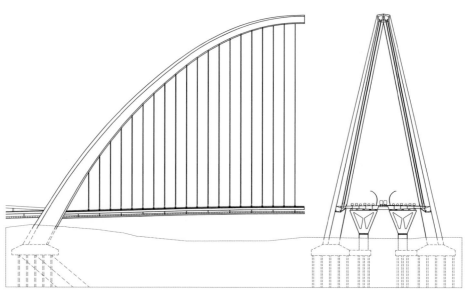

West Elevation and Section

How do we forge a relationship to the landscape? This question was a constant in our work on Qala Alti, both in the overall framework and in the realm of ideas. Our response is not about the willful personal impulse. It is plainly about a conversation with the side of the mountain. Dan Kaplan

Both the planning strategy and the visual expression of the Qala Alti Hotel Spa in Azerbaijan derive from the immediate context: the pleated rock of the Caucasus Mountains. The architecture, in turns, emerges from the horizontal ground plane, grows from the vertical rock, and floats above the land. The resulting forms communicate with the terrain, playfully questioning and revealing facets of the relationship between architecture and landscape.

Azerbaijan gained (or regained) its independence from the USSR in 1991. Rich in oil and natural gas, the country is promoting economic growth by reinvigorating its tourism industry. In the Communist era, Qala Alti was a state-sponsored and highly prized vacation destination for the Soviet Union. Close to the capital city of Baku, graced with natural hot springs and healing waters, the area has long been a place for health-related travel. The new 180-room hotel, spa, and recreational facility is a touchstone project for the revitalization.

The site, on the edge of the Caucasus Mountains, is a landscape rich in history. It is located just below the historic Chirax Castle, part of an ancient mountain fortification, and overlooks a plain that abuts the Caspian Sea, an important early farming belt and trading route. Chirax Castle is a remnant of a chain of fortifications built to defend the plain.

The hotel buildings cascade down the side of the mountain, interweaving different program elements with the landscape. The site organization produces distinct pockets of activity that negotiate the extreme topography. The large hotel spa is at the top of the site; entrance to the complex is at the bottom, where guests are greeted by an entertainment building with an infinity pool and seemingly natural brook. Nestled along the road that leads from the entertainment building to the hotel are villas that grow from the landscape and tree houses that hover above it. The various structures serve to propose and juxtapose different relationships between landscape and architecture. The road itself creates a moment of architectural clarity. The angular nooks and crannies of the mountains transform into architecture, and the green edges of the landscape merge into the hotel complex.

A narrative of water guides guests through the hotel buildings. A fountain, representing healing waters, becomes a stream within the hotel spa; it flows through a territory of spa treatments, gathering spaces, gardens, and recreational facilities. The water takes on other forms as it descends through the naturalistic landscape. Therapeutic landscapes near the hotel—a grotto, a mud/hot springs area—transition to more active uses: a lawn for tai chi, an amphitheater for larger gatherings, and a geothermal pond. Even farther down the hill are athletic recreation spaces, including tennis courts, rock climbing area, and outdoor adventure area. At the base, in the recreation building, is a large communal pool.

The architecture of the hotel spa conveys the forces of twisting rock merging into decaying castle and into landscape. We developed three distinct typologies to exemplify different aspects of these relationships. The first draws from the rock face: the architecture appears to emerge fluidly from the mountain. The second hovers above the landscape: it is clearly separate, architectonic and crafted, and emphasizes the separation between the built and the natural. The third is an extension of the landscape: the ground plane peels up into angled sides and occupiable green roofs.

Used separately and in combination, these typologies express the character of the different site elements. The podiums of the entertainment building and the hotel spa grow out of the rock; they emerge from the mountain face and create a solid base. The rooftop bar/pavilion at the top of the hotel, by contrast, hovers on pilotis. The hotel spa building scissors down the mountain, formalizing the change in topography. It simultaneously issues from the side of the mountain, emerges from the ground, and floats above the site.

The material nature of the facade echoes the folded rocks of the Caucasus Mountains. A thin module of striated brick enhances the complex chiseled geometry of the carved-out rooms. The balconies incorporate integral planters, and the windows look over the fertile plain and out to the Caspian Sea.

We directed our efforts toward engaging Qala Alti with its site, a landscape that is geologic in scale and historic in scope. The permutations of architectonic form trace the character of the mountainous context while continually juxtaposing elements of landscape and built form. The site organization is choreographed to offer experiences of ambiguity and experiences of clarity, to blur boundaries and celebrate them.

Fifth Floor Plan

Fourth Floor Plan

Third Floor Plan

Second Floor Plan

Ground Floor Plan

Site

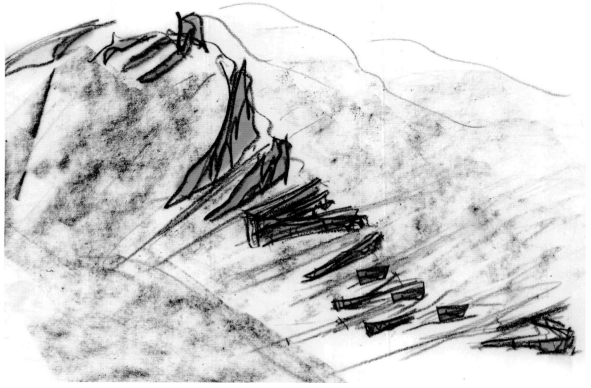

Concept Sketch

Facade Study: Structure

Facade Study: Material

Facade Study: Greening

Construction: December 2013

Senior Partners
Gerard F. X. Geier II, FAIA, FIIDA, LEED
Sudhir S. Jambhekar, FAIA, RIBA, LEED
Daniel J. Kaplan, FAIA, LEED
Sylvia J. Smith, FAIA, LEED
Mark E. Strauss, FAIA, AICP/PP, LEED

Partners
Heidi L. Blau, FAIA, LEED
Tim Milam, AIA, LEED
John Schuyler, AIA, LEED

Founding Principal
Bruce S. Fowle, FAIA, LEED

Project Credits

Introduction/Nature as Site

SAP Americas Headquarters Expansion,
David Sundberg/Esto (p2, 10, 12)
Center for Global Conservation,
David Sundberg/Esto (p4, 6, 8, 14)

Center for Global Conservation

Partner-in-Charge: Sylvia Smith
Project Manager: Susan Masi
Project Architect: Tom Fox, Paul Kim
Project Designer: Frank D. MacNelly
Team: Aurisbel T. Banny, Guy Geier,
Rodney Hammer, Nicholas Hollot,
Heng-Choong Leong, Daniel Piselli,
Alexander Redfern, Monika Sarac

Structural Engineer:
DeSimone Consulting Engineers
Consulting Engineer:
Kallen & Lemelson, LLP
Geotechnical Engineer: Langan
Engineering, Environmental, Surveying
and Landscape Architecture, D.P.C.
Landscape Engineer: HM White
Site Architects
Lighting: Brandston Partnership
Elevator: Van Deusen & Associates
Signage: Whitehouse & Company
A/V: KP Johnson & Associates
Photography: David Sundberg/Esto

City Regenerative: Nordhavnen

Partner-in-Charge: Dan Kaplan,
Mark Strauss
Project Director: Stephan Dallendorfer
Project Designer: Toby Snyder, Alvaro
Quintana, Brandon Massey
Team: Vikrant Dalvi, Ilana Judah,
Jessica Wyman

Urban Design: architectureRED
Landscape Architect: Starr Whitehouse
Landscape Architects and Planners
Environmental: Buro Happold
Consulting Engineers
Prefabrication/Modular: Global
Building Modules, Inc., David
Wallance Architect

SAP Americas
Headquarters Expansion

Partner-in-Charge: Guy Geier
Design Partner: Bruce Fowle
Project Director: John Schuyler
Project Architect, Senior Designer:
Gustavo Rodriguez
Senior Designer, Interior: Sara Agrest
Team: Aurisbel T. Banny, Margherita
Bartorelli, Hsin Yi Chang, Lisa
Cheung, Nathan Herber, Robert
Hills, Ervin Hirsan, Robert D. Lanni
Jr., Woo-Hyoung Lee, Brenda May,
Alvaro Quintero, Thomas M. Scarda,
Stephanie Schreiber, Louise Smith,
Nicholas Tocheff, Joseph White

Structural Engineer:
Severud Associates
MEP Engineer, Fire Protection:
Flack+Kurtz Engineers
Landscape Architect: Wallace
Roberts & Todd, LLC
Site/Civil/Geotechnical Engineer:
Advanced Geoservices
Telecommunications: Telnet
Consulting, Inc.
Security: ADT Advance Integration
Acoustic, A/V: Harvey Marshall Berling
Associates
Vertical Transportation: Van Deusen
& Associates
Exterior Wall: Heitmann & Associates

Lighting: S & S Lighting Design
Green Roof: Roofscapes, Inc.
Sustainable Design: YRG
Sustainability Consultants
Photography: David Sundberg/Esto

Sheikh Rashid bin Saeed Crossing

Partner-in-Charge: Sudhir Jambhekar
Project Manager: Edward Mayer
Project Architect: Daniel Piselli
Project Designer: Colin Montoute
Team: Nobuhiko Arai, Elizabeth
Gilligan, Soren Graae, George Kewin,
Leonid Kravchenko, Singjoy Liang,
Ayman Makeen, Steve Miller, Naomi
Ocko, Joseph Reyes, Gerard Sambets
Jr., Yasmeen Shamsudden, Na Young
Shim, Yonghyun Yu

Landscape Architect: W Architecture
& Landscape Architecture, LLC
Lighting: AWA Lighting Designers
Electrical Engineer: Services Design
Technology International
Photography: Jock Pottle (p58)

Qala Alti Hotel Spa

Partner-in-Charge: Dan Kaplan
Project Manager: Fatin Anlar
Project Designer: Gustavo Rodriguez
Team: Yu Ying Goh, Carol Hsiung,
Munhee Kang, William McLoughlin,
Seiji Watanabe, Beth Wells Gensemer

Landscape Architect: LandDesign
Interior Design: 3R Design Factory
MEP, Structural Engineer: RC-AZ
Photography: Coe Hoeksema (p65)

Published by
ORO Editions
Publisher: Gordon Goff
Copyright © 2014 by FXFOWLE Architects, LLP
ISBN: 978-1-935935-63-6
10 09 08 07 06 5 4 3 2 1 First Edition

Consulting Editor: Andrea Monfried
Text: Liz Campbell Kelly
Design: ORO Editions
FXFOWLE Monograph Team: Guy Geier, Amanda Abel, Karen Bookatz, and Brien McDaniel
Color Separations and Printing: ORO Group Ltd.
Production: Usana Shadday and Alexandria Nazar
Printed in China

This book was printed and bound using a variety of sustainable manufacturing processes
and materials including, aqueous-based varnish, VOC- and formaldehyde-free glues, and
phthalate-free laminations. The text is printed using offset sheetfed lithographic printing
process in 5 color on 140 gsm woodfree art paper and 157 gsm matt art paper with an off-line
spot gloss varnish applied to all photographs.

ORO Editions makes a continuous effort to minimize the overall carbon footprint of its
publications. As part of this goal, ORO Editions, in association with Global ReLeaf, arranges
to plant trees to replace those used in the manufacturing of the paper produced for its books.
Global ReLeaf is an international campaign run by American Forests, one of the world's
oldest nonprofit conservation organizations. Global ReLeaf is American Forests' education
and action program that helps individuals, organizations, agencies, and corporations improve
the local and global environment by planting and caring for trees.

Library of Congress Cataloging-in-Publication Data:
Available upon request